Unscripted

Things I didn't plan to note down

Prachi Kothari

Made with ❤ on the BookLeaf Publishing Platform
www.bookleafpub.in
www.bookleafpub.com

Dedication

For every lesson disguised as love, every scar that became strength, every joy that felt like home, and every moment of uncertainty that led me here.

I am grateful—for the journey, the discovery, the pain, the hope, and the endless becoming.

Preface

Life doesn't come with a script. It unfolds in ways we never imagined, slipping between the cracks of our plans, leaving us with moments that shape us forever.

This book is a collection of those moments—stories I never thought I'd write, lessons I never thought I'd learn, and emotions I never planned to feel. It's about the unplanned, the unexpected, and the unscripted—the raw, unfiltered experiences that have made me who I am today.

I grew up believing in plans, in having the right answers, in following the path that made sense. But life had other ideas. It threw detours my way, challenged my beliefs, and led me to places I never thought I'd go. Some of these moments were beautiful, others were painful, but all of them were real. And with each experience, I found pieces of myself I didn't even know were missing.

This book isn't a guide. It's not a roadmap or a lesson in how to live life "correctly." It's a reflection—a collection of stories, thoughts, and realizations that came to me when I least expected them. Some are funny, some are deep, some are messy, and some still feel unfinished. But that's the thing about life—it's always evolving, and we're always learning.

If you've ever felt lost, uncertain, or like your life isn't going the way you planned—this book is for you. I hope, somewhere in these pages, you find a bit of yourself, a bit of comfort, and a reminder that sometimes, the best things in life happen when we stop trying to control the script.

Here's to embracing the *unscripted.*

Acknowledgements

Writing *Unscripted* has been an experience as raw and unpredictable as the stories within it. It is a piece of my heart, a reflection of moments that have shaped me, and none of it would have been possible without the people who have stood by me—sometimes knowingly, sometimes unknowingly.

To my family—thank you for being my first-hand storytellers, for giving me the space to dream, and for grounding me when I needed it the most. Your love, presence and support has been my foundation.

To my partner—for being my anchor, my safe space, and my constant.

To my friends—you are the unscripted joys of my life. The ones who have laughed with me, cried with me, and reminded me that life doesn't need to be figured out all at once. Your presence has made my chaos feel less chaotic, and for that, I am endlessly grateful.

To the people who have been part of my journey—whether for a lifetime or a fleeting moment—thank you. You have been my teachers in ways I never expected.

Some of you offered warmth, some of you offered lessons, and some of you offered challenges that forced me to grow. Each of you, in your own way, has shaped these pages.

And finally, to you—the reader. Thank you for picking up this book.

Whether you found it by chance or intention, I hope it speaks to you in some way. I hope it reminds you that life doesn't always go as planned, but sometimes, the unplanned moments are the ones that make us who we are.

With all my heart,
Prachi

Contents

—

2

Part 1

Beginnings & Becoming

Every story starts somewhere—not always with a grand moment, but often in the quiet, unassuming spaces of life. In this section, I revisit the fragments of my early years, the first lessons I never realized I was learning, and the small, defining moments that shaped me.

These are the stories of childhood wonder, of discovering who I was before the world told me who to be. They are about the innocence of first dreams, the weight of unspoken fears, and the slow but certain realization that change is the only constant.

Here lies the beginning—not just of this book, but of me.

Cracks & Confessions

As a child, I often found myself exploring the quiet corners of our home, drawn by an insatiable curiosity. One afternoon, while my parents were away, I discovered my mother's cherished jewellery box. In my eagerness, I accidentally broke it. Panic-stricken, I attempted to repair the damage with glue, hoping to conceal my mistake.

Despite my efforts, the fracture remained evident, and when my mother noticed, I denied any involvement. Her disappointment was palpable, and in that moment, I realized that the weight of dishonesty far exceeded the consequences of admitting my fault. This experience taught me the profound value of owning up to my actions and the liberation that comes with truthfulness.

"In silent halls, my footsteps crept, a child's quest where secrets slept.
Fingers grazed a treasured find, a box adorned, with stories lined.
A sudden slip, a muted crash, fragments lay amidst the

ash.
Heart aflutter, guilt awoke, a precious heirloom I had broke.

With trembling hands, I sought to mend, to hide the truth, to thwart the end.
But cracks, like whispers, still appeared, betraying all that I had feared.
Her eyes inquired, mine withdrew, a feeble lie, a tangled skew.
Yet mothers sense the unsaid word, and in her silence, truth was heard.

From that day forth, I came to see, the strength that lies in honesty.
For though mistakes may mar our past, confession's light is unsurpassed."

———

The Math of It All

*There are lessons that stay with us forever—tiny ripples
that shape the ocean of who we become. For me, one of
those moments was realizing that numbers, no matter
how hard I tried, would never feel like home.*

*Sitting in a classroom, lost in equations that blurred into
nothingness, I felt small, incapable, and utterly out of
place. But what I didn't know then was that this
discomfort would eventually lead me to words—the place
where I truly belonged. It took years to understand that
not every strength is found in the expected places, and
that failing at one thing does not mean failing at life.*

———

"They said numbers were the language of the universe,
but they never spoke to me.
They twisted into knots,
coiled like questions I couldn't untangle,
mocking me with their certainty.

I sat there, frozen,
as the teacher scribbled answers I could never find,

and the room spun with calculations
that never quite added up in my mind.

And for years, I let them convince me—
that my worth was measured in equations,
that a misplaced decimal could rewrite my future.
But here I am, writing my own language,
one that doesn't need formulas to make sense,
one that feels like home.

Because not all of us are meant for numbers.
Some of us are meant for words."

—

Unruly & Unapologetic

Some rules don't come written in books, yet they are spoken with such certainty that they almost feel like the truth. At a wedding in my teens, an elderly uncle casually told me that "good girls" don't leave their hair open—that looking presentable meant being neatly tied up. It was meant to be advice, but to me, it felt like a quiet command. One that I had no reason to follow.

———

"They called it decorum, I called it a cage.
They said a girl should be polished, contained—
but I had never seen beauty in smallness.

So I let the wind play with my hair,
let it dance against my face,
unruly, untamed, unbothered.

For years, they tried to tuck away our wildness,
fold us into neatness, into silence.

But I was never meant to be tied down—
not by hair, not by expectations, not by rules

that made no space for who I wanted to be."

—

Conversations That Changed Us

Growing up in a time when friendships were often seen through the lens of tradition, I found myself in a quiet battle against generational beliefs. My landline phone would ring, and if it was a girl calling, it was just another conversation. But if it was a boy, questions would follow —not accusations, just innocent curiosity.

My Dadi (Papa's Mum), with all her love, would wonder aloud why boys were calling her granddaughter. But the beauty of her curiosity was that it wasn't rigid. Once I explained to her how school worked, how friendships were not bound by gender, she embraced it all effortlessly. And in the process, we found a bond of our own—one that lasted late into the night, sharing stories, laughter, and a newfound understanding of each other.

—

"We often assume that the old will remain old, that their beliefs will never shift, and their traditions will always weigh heavy. But sometimes, all it takes is a conversation.

A quiet exchange of perspectives, a gentle breaking of inherited notions. My Dadi could have clung to what she had always known. Instead, she chose to listen. And in listening, she gave me the space to be who I was—without judgment, without restraint.

Not all walls are built to keep you in; some are waiting to be turned into doorways. And not all traditions exist to chain you; some simply need to be dusted off and seen in a new light."

—

The Day My Body Spoke

Some changes announce themselves with a bang; others arrive quietly, leaving you to piece together their meaning. At 11, I didn't know what it meant to grow into myself. But that day, my body whispered a truth I wasn't ready to hear yet—it had begun.

———

"It arrived unannounced, a quiet stain on my pajamas, a secret my body had been keeping until now. My mother guided me through it, her voice steady, her hands sure. But inside, I felt lost, like something irreversible had happened. I didn't understand.

No one had prepared me for this.

Was I broken? Was this normal? Why did it feel like something had been taken from me when, in truth, something had been given?

For days, I felt like a stranger in my own skin. My body was shifting, shaping itself into something new. I saw it

in the mirror, in the way clothes fit differently, in the
way I became aware of things I had never noticed before.
The weight of change settled into my bones, and I carried
it in silence.

But as time passed, I learned. This was not a betrayal—it
was an initiation. A quiet, sacred transformation. The
same cycle that pained me would one day give me the
power to create life, to nurture, to sustain. What felt like
a loss was, in truth, a gift.

I still resent the pain. The exhaustion. The way the world
sometimes treats it like a burden. But I do not resent
what it means. My body spoke to me that day, and
though I did not understand it then, I do now—this was
never a curse.

It was a crown."

———

Why I Stopped Cycling

Some lessons arrive too soon. Not in the form of books or lectures, but in a quiet shift of the air, in the way a moment can turn from ordinary to something else entirely. Sometimes, fear does not come with a warning —it finds you when you least expect it.

———

"You were just 10, waiting for a friend with your cycle on a quiet afternoon, believing the world was still as safe as it had always been. But then you felt a shadow, a presence that did not belong. And suddenly, the air was different.

A man in a pink shirt on a scooter stopped next to you and smiled as he unzipped his pants while jerking off to your innocence.

Your hands gripped the handlebars, your heart beat against your ribs, and something inside you knew— *you need torun.* And so you did.

You pedalled hard, turned sharp corners, trying to

outrun a feeling you didn't yet have words for. When he didn't stop following, you threw your dear cycle in the middle of nowhere and ran for your life.

When you reached home drenched in sweat and fear, your parents asked what had happened. You told them part of the truth, that a man had followed you, but not all of it. Not the part that made your skin crawl, that made you feel smaller than you had ever felt before. Because you didn't know if you could. Because something in you feared that saying it out loud might make it worse.

I wish I could reach back through time and hold your trembling hands. Tell you that the shame was never yours to carry. That fear should never have been your burden. That your voice is not a crime, and your silence is not protection.

But most of all, I want you to know—you were not wrong to be afraid. You were wronged. And no matter how much time has passed, no matter how many others have walked this road—*your story matters.*"

Part 2

Weight of Undeclared Expectations

Some expectations are handed to you with a grand announcement—like being told to score well in exams or marry *at the right time*. Others sneak in quietly, settling on your shoulders before you even realize they're there. Like the unspoken rule that you must always be *the responsible one*, or that saying *no* makes you ungrateful.

Nobody asked if I wanted to carry these invisible burdens. They just appeared, wrapped in tradition, love, guilt—sometimes all three at once (a particularly suffocating combination). I spent years trying to live up to roles I never auditioned for, mistaking obligation for purpose, assuming that disappointing people was the worst thing I could do.

Spoiler alert: it wasn't.

This part is about those silent pressures—the ones that shaped me, boxed me in, and eventually, the ones I learned to shrug off. They're about the guilt of letting go, the relief of choosing myself, and the realization that life doesn't come with a fixed script. Turns out, you can rip up the old one and write your own.

Loosen the Straps, Not the Standards

Some women carry the weight of expectations so deeply that they pass it down like an heirloom. They whisper corrections, impose rules, and tighten the very shackles that once bound them. But hypocrisy has a way of revealing itself—sometimes over drinks and hushed complaints, sometimes in the casual policing of a visible bra strap.

—

"She leaned in, her voice low but firm—'Your bra strap is showing. Be more careful in public.'

I watched her walk back to her table, where she laughed over drinks, venting about her husband and in-laws. The irony clung to the air like perfume.

Isn't it strange? How women, already burdened by expectations, sometimes become the enforcers of them? How they pass down rules they once resented? How they hush a young girl's clothing while drowning their own sorrows in secrets?

That day, I realized—some rules were made to be broken. And some women were never truly free."

19

—

On Being the Firstborn

I don't remember the day I officially became an elder sister, but I do remember when I realized what it meant. It wasn't just about holding a tiny hand or sharing my chocolates—it was about responsibility, about setting an example, about always being the "mature one." If my brother made a mistake, I was asked why I didn't stop him. If he cried, I was asked why I didn't take care of him better. And if I ever dared to cry myself, I was reminded that I was the elder one—stronger, wiser, the one who had to hold it all together.

I was only 9 when I felt the weight of this responsibility crush me for the first time. We were at a hill station, on a family trip with our parents, relatives, and cousins. Horse riding was the highlight of the day, and as our ride ended, they got my little brother down first. Before I could even get off and check on him, he was gone. Just vanished.

Panic set in like wildfire. My parents, relatives—everyone —scattered in different directions, calling out his name, searching frantically. But he was nowhere to be found. I stood there, frozen, my heart pounding with guilt. I was his elder sister. I should have been watching. I should have been more careful. The weight of those 'should haves' made it hard to breathe.

An hour later, just as fear was turning into devastation, we found him. Sitting at a restaurant's reception, eyes glued to the TV, blissfully unaware of the chaos he had caused. I wanted to yell at him. I wanted to hug him. Instead, I just stood there, relief washing over me in waves, realizing that when you are the elder one, the instinct to protect never truly leaves you. It is not something you are taught—it is something you just **become***."*

———

"I have carried his weight longer than he has walked,
not in my arms, but in my heart.
Every scraped knee, every lost shoe, every tear,
somehow, always felt like my fault.

And that day, when he disappeared into thin air,
I didn't just lose him for an hour,
I lost myself to guilt.
The fear wrapped around my ribs,
tight as the expectations I had unknowingly inherited.

Elder sisters don't get to panic.

Elder sisters don't get to be children.
But when we found him—safe, smiling,
watching TV like the world hadn't fallen apart—
I realized something.

Being an elder sibling isn't about always getting it right.
It's about always showing up,
always caring,
always holding on—even when they don't realize you
are."

———

You Are Invited

Weddings are a social battleground for most of the young people, especially for women. The moment you walk in, the questions start. "Beta, tumhari kab hai?" If you have a job, "Accha, but what about shaadi?" If you're dating, "Arre, kitna time logi?" If you're married, "Good news kab de rahi ho?" A woman's milestones are never her own—they are a public checklist, waiting to be ticked off by everyone except her.

There's an unspoken urgency in their voices, as if happiness has an expiration date. As if dreams need to be balanced like a precarious house of cards—one wrong move, and the whole thing collapses. And in that moment, standing under the weight of flashing cameras and expectations, you begin to wonder: Is there something wrong with me? Am I running out of time?

But time is not slipping away. It is being stolen—by every voice that tells a woman what she should be instead of asking her who she wants to be.

—

"*You are invited—*

To the wedding, to the gathering, to the dinner where your choices are laid out like dishes on the table. Where your age is counted more than your achievements. Where your worth is measured by the weight of a ring on your finger.

You are invited—

To smile politely at intrusive questions. To dodge unsolicited advice. To explain, yet again, why your life doesn't follow their timeline.

You are invited—

To doubt yourself. To go home and stare at the ceiling, wondering if you are, in fact, behind.

But here's my RSVP—**No, thank you.**

I am not on borrowed time. I am not a glass slipper waiting for a perfect fit. I am not an invitation for you to dissect my choices.

My life is not a wedding hall conversation. It is mine,

and it is enough."

—

Friendly Unfriending

Friendships are supposed to be a safe space—until you realize in some friendships, you're only welcome when you're smiling. You're expected to show up, reply on time, and never go missing. If you take a step back to breathe, they call you distant. If you don't have the energy to listen today, they say you've changed.

But here's the thing—sometimes, even the happiest friend gets tired. Sometimes, even the listener needs to be heard. And sometimes, the strongest ones aren't pushing people away; they're just trying to hold themselves together.

The problem is, when you become the person who always brings light into the room, people forget you, too, need a window sometimes.

———

"*Where have you been?* they ask.
Not in an *I-miss-you* way, but in an *I-need-you* way.
Not because they want to check on you, but because they need to unload.

They mistake your silence for anger.
They mistake your absence for neglect.
They never stop to think—maybe, just maybe, you are
carrying something too heavy to share.
But friendships should be more than borrowed
shoulders.

I am not a therapist.
I am not a hotline you dial when your world is falling
apart but forget when mine is.
Some days, I will disappear.
Not because I don't care, but because I need to take care
—of me."

—

Party Pooper's Guilt

There is an unspoken rule in every social circle—the more you show up, the more you belong. The late nights, the inside jokes, the endless plans that stretch from one weekend to the next. And while being part of something is beautiful, so is stepping back when your soul asks for it.

It's not about avoiding people. It's about choosing where your energy flows. Some nights, the music feels right, the laughter feels easy, and you're the last one to leave. Other nights, your heart craves quiet—a book, a movie, a pause before the world pulls you back in.

Saying yes to people should never mean saying no to yourself.

———

"Some nights, I dance under neon lights.
Some nights, I sip tea under fairy lights.
Some days, I crave the sound of a crowded room.
Some days, I need the silence of my own space.

Neither is an escape.
Both are a choice.
Belonging is not about always showing up.
It's about knowing when to step in and when to step
back."

—

29

Spaces Between Us – What We Share, What We Hold Back

There's a silent expectation between parents and children—one that whispers, "Tell me everything." They want to know your dreams, your struggles, the things that keep you up at night. But what they don't always realize is that some truths feel too heavy to share. Not because of shame or secrecy, but because you don't know how they'll carry it.

As a teenager, I held back—not out of defiance, but out of protection. I didn't want my mistakes to become their worries. I didn't want their disapproval to become my self-doubt. So I measured my words, filtered my confessions, and sometimes, I let silence hold what I wasn't ready to say.

Growing up is realizing that love doesn't always mean full disclosure. Sometimes, it means creating a soft distance—not to deceive, but to preserve.

—

"Not every secret is a rebellion.
Not every silence is a lie.
Some things we share,
Some things we carry alone.
And maybe, that's okay."

—

Part 3

Love, Loss & Everything In Between

Love isn't always what we expect it to be. It isn't just grand gestures, poetic confessions, or a story that always ends with "happily ever after." Sometimes, love is quiet. Sometimes, it's fleeting. Sometimes, it's found in the most unexpected places—a stranger who goes the extra mile, a child who understands your silence, or even in the painful goodbye that teaches you the most about yourself.

Loss, too, reshapes us. The heartbreaks that feel like they will break us often lead us to a better version of ourselves. The friendships that fade without closure remind us that some people are meant to be chapters, not the whole book. And yet, through every loss, love finds a way back—sometimes in the form of self-love,

sometimes in the form of a person you never saw
coming.

This section is about all of it—the love that stayed, the
love that left, and the love that found its way back in
ways I never expected.

17. First Time I Said "I Love You"

Love is often thought of as something we give to others —a confession to a partner, a reassurance to a friend, a promise to family. But before I ever said it to anyone else, I said it to myself.

As a child, I saw my parents exchange those three words, and though I didn't fully understand their weight, I knew they meant something special. One day, standing in front of the mirror, I wondered—could I say them to myself? Could I mean them?

The reflection staring back wasn't just me; it was someone else too. A version of myself that felt like a safe space, a quiet companion. I'd gaze into my own eyes, whisper "I love you," and somehow, it felt true. I wasn't alone—I had me.

——

"I told myself I love you before I ever said it to anyone else.

In the mirror, I saw someone who never left, never judged, never wavered.
She was always there, through every phase, every doubt, every stumble.
And I still love her—more than I ever did before."

—

18. Losing Someone Who Is Still Alive

Friendships aren't supposed to end in silence. There's supposed to be a fight, a confrontation, a reason. But sometimes, people leave without a word, without an explanation, without even the courtesy of a goodbye.

She was my friend for 8 years. We had been through heartbreaks, career struggles, late-night rants, and inside jokes that no one else understood. And then, one day, she was gone. Just like that. No message, no closure—just a void where she used to be.

I waited. And waited. I sent messages, apologized for things I didn't even know I had done. I checked her last-seen, scrolled through old conversations, hoping to find a clue. But there was nothing. Just unanswered texts and the sharp sting of being erased from someone's life.

I still see her sometimes—smiling in someone else's pictures, living a life that no longer includes me. And maybe that's the worst part of losing someone who's still alive. The knowing. The watching. The quiet grief of an unfinished goodbye.

—

37

"There was no final fight, no closure, no explanation. Just the slow realization that I had been written out of a story I thought we were still telling together."

—

19. Extra Miles for an Extra Bite

Not all strangers remain strangers. Some, even in fleeting moments, leave behind warmth that lingers.

That night, I was exhausted. Craving a burger that was nowhere close to my usual route home. I hesitated before asking, expecting an annoyed response, a reminder of extra charges, or just a refusal. But instead, the cab driver smiled and said, "Koi baat nahi, le chalte hain."

He drove in silence, taking a longer route just so I could indulge in something small yet comforting. And when I offered him a share of my meal, he accepted—not just the food, but the moment. That's when he told me his story.

He had lost his family. His life had no defined purpose anymore, no one to return home to. He wasn't driving for the money; he was driving for the company. Meeting new people, sharing a few moments of kindness—it was his way of filling the silence of his life.

I got more than a burger that day. I got a reminder that sometimes, the kindest souls are the ones carrying the heaviest burdens. And that even in passing, we can be

———

"Not all detours delay us. Some take us exactly where we need to be—towards a fleeting moment of kindness, a shared meal, a reminder that even in our loneliness, we are never truly alone."

———

What I Thought I Wanted vs. What I Actually Needed

When we're younger, our idea of love is often shaped by movies, books, and fleeting infatuations. We believe love should be effortless, filled with grand gestures, endless admiration, and someone who mirrors our thoughts and feelings. I once thought I needed a partner who would worship my art, validate my every belief, and never challenge my world. I longed for a love that felt like a dream.

But over time, I realized that true love isn't about constant agreement or uncritical admiration. It's about growth, about being with someone who expands your world instead of simply living in it. Love isn't just about romance—it's about being challenged, understood, and supported in ways you never knew you needed.

———

"When I was younger,
I dreamt of a love that dripped in poetry,
of someone who would trace constellations on my skin
and whisper verses into my tired bones.

I wanted a love that clapped the loudest
when I spoke,
that echoed my thoughts
without ever questioning them.

I thought I needed a lover
who lived in colours and metaphors,
someone who would paint my mornings golden
and sketch my sorrows into something beautiful.

I thought love was someone nodding,
always nodding,
agreeing that my world was the only world worth living
in.

But love—real love—
is not a gallery of admiration,
not a mirror that only reflects what you want to see.
It is the hand that pulls you out of your own canvas,
the voice that tells you when your colours are bleeding,
when your lines need softening.

I found love in someone
who did not just praise me
but pushed me.
Who did not just agree with me
but challenged me.

Who was not only an artist
but an anchor—
steady, unwavering, real.
I thought I needed a love that romanticized me.
But what I truly needed
was a love that made me better."

———

Littlest Guardian of My Heart

Friendships come in all shapes and sizes, but the most unexpected ones are often the purest. Who would have thought that a child—24 years younger than me—would understand me better than most adults? It doesn't feel like I'm talking to a kid; it feels like I'm talking to someone who just gets me.

There was a day when silent tears found their way down my face. I didn't say a word, but he noticed. And instead of asking what was wrong, instead of offering empty reassurances, he simply started cracking random jokes. No questions, no expectations—just warmth, just comfort. Sometimes, love isn't in grand gestures or lifelong promises. Sometimes, it's in a child's instinct to protect you, in the way they hold space for you without even realizing it.

—

"Love doesn't always arrive in familiar forms. Sometimes, it comes in small hands, easy laughter, and the quiet understanding of someone who sees you, truly sees you—even when you're trying to hide."

—

Part 4

Fear, Failure & Falling Forward

We are taught to fear failure, to see it as an end rather than a turning point. But what if failure is just a pause—a moment of redirection rather than defeat? This section is about the times I stumbled, the moments of uncertainty, and the fears that almost held me back.

From career confusion to dreams that didn't materialize, from burning rotis to moving cities with nothing but faith, these stories are a reminder that falling isn't the opposite of progress—it's a part of it.

Here, I write about the things that didn't go as planned, the lessons I resisted but needed, and the ways I learned to embrace fear instead of letting it define me. Because every failure carries a hidden gift: the chance to rise again, stronger and wiser than before.

Not Every Passion Becomes a Profession

Some dreams are meant to be lived, not pursued. There was a time I thought theatre was my calling—that I was meant to stand under the spotlight, perform, and make a life out of it. But not every passion is meant to become a profession. Sometimes, it is simply meant to be something that brings you joy, without the pressure of success or failure.

—

"There was a time when I believed the stage was where I belonged. The thrill of performing, the rush of emotions, the way a character could become a part of me—it felt like magic. I thought it was my path, my purpose, the thing I was meant to do for the rest of my life.

But dreams, like theatre, have their own plot twists.

The more I pursued it, the more I realized that loving something and excelling at it were two different things. I wasn't the best performer in the room, and deep down, I knew it. I could feel the weight of expectations—both my own and those around me. What if I wasn't good enough? What if the thing I loved turned into something that drained me instead of fulfilling me?

Letting go of a dream you once held so tightly is a strange kind of heartbreak. But over time, I understood something important—passion doesn't have to be a profession to be meaningful.

Theatre still moves me. I still get lost in performances, still feel my heart race when I watch a brilliant play. But now, I enjoy it without the pressure of making it my life. Some loves are meant to be kept for ourselves, without turning them into a job, a responsibility, or a burden.

Not every passion is meant to be chased. Some are simply meant to be cherished."

—

The Clueless Years – Taking a Leap of Faith

It's a strange kind of loneliness in not knowing what's next. After my master's, I was stuck in a limbo—too many failed entrance exams behind me, too much uncertainty ahead. I had no clear direction, no "perfect" plan, just a feeling that I wanted to write.

And so, I took a leap of faith. This is about trusting yourself even when the path isn't clear—because sometimes, clarity comes only after you've started walking.

—

"There are few things scarier than staring at a blank page —not knowing where to begin, what to say, or if the words will ever come together. That's exactly how my life felt after my Master's.

I had done everything I was 'supposed' to do. Yet, one failed entrance exam after another left me questioning everything. What now? What next? The world had no answers, and for a while, neither did I.

But amid all the confusion, one thing remained unchanged—I loved expressing myself through words. Writing felt like home. It wasn't a secure career choice, not the kind of profession that people around me would call 'stable'. But something in me whispered that I should give it a shot. So, I did.

I started writing, unsure if it would lead anywhere. The first few steps were wobbly. Self-doubt was louder than confidence. But slowly, one opportunity led to another. And before I knew it, the thing I once questioned had become my career, my purpose.

Looking back, I realize that certainty is overrated. No one really knows where a road will lead before they take the first step. Sometimes, the best things in life come from trusting yourself when the future is a blur. After all, every great story starts with a blank page—you just have to be brave enough to start writing."

Courage to Move Cities & My Father's Belief in Me

Leaving behind everything familiar is never easy—especially when society expects you to stay put, to follow a set path, to not stray too far. But my father, the man who has always believed in independence beyond just finances, told me something that changed everything: You have to be independent in all ways—physically, emotionally, mentally. Only then can you truly **stand on your own.**

With his belief in me, I took the leap and moved cities. This is about fear, freedom, and the courage it takes to build a life on your own terms.

———

"I still remember the moment I placed the last bag in my new apartment. The silence around me felt unfamiliar, a reminder that I had truly left home. For the first time in my life, I was on my own—not just for a trip or a temporary escape, but to build something new from scratch.

In our society, a woman moving out alone, especially in her late 20s, isn't exactly the norm. It comes with a thousand unsaid questions—*Why does she need to? What's wrong with staying home?* But my father never asked those questions. Instead, he told me, *Independence isn't just about earning your own money; it's about standing on your own feet in every way possible.*

His words stayed with me through the nights I missed home, through the loneliness of setting up a new life, through the doubts that crept in when things got hard. But then, one day, I realized something—this city no longer felt foreign. I had found my own rhythm, my own people, my own corners of comfort.

Moving away wasn't just about changing locations; it was about finding the strength to create a life that felt like mine. And every time I second-guess my decisions, I remember the quiet confidence in my father's voice, reminding me that I was always meant to stand on my own."

—

How I Kept Moving

For as long as I can remember, I have believed in therapy —not as a last resort but as a way to understand myself better. I started young, at a time when mental health was still a whispered conversation, something people either ignored or feared.

But to me, seeking help was never a weakness. It was a choice to heal, to move forward, to not let my struggles define me. Therapy has given me clarity, taught me resilience, and, most importantly, reminded me that I am not alone. This is about the quiet strength it takes to keep going, even when the road feels endless.

———

"There was a time when my thoughts felt like a tangled mess—questions without answers, emotions I didn't know how to name. I would sit with the weight of it all, wondering if I would ever feel lighter. And then, one day, I walked into my first therapy session.

At first, it was uncomfortable, like standing in front of a mirror that showed every part of me—the good, the messy, the scared. But slowly, it became my safe space. A space where I could put words to my fears, where healing wasn't about 'fixing' anything but about understanding myself.

Therapy didn't change my life overnight. What it did was give me the tools to navigate it better. It taught me that my struggles didn't make me weak, that feeling deeply wasn't a flaw, and that even in the hardest moments, there was always a way forward.

I still have difficult days, but now I know I don't have to face them alone. And if there's one thing therapy has given me above all else, it's this: the courage to keep going, even when I don't have all the answers yet."

—

Aroma of Burnt Rotis

Cooking was never something I looked forward to. As a child, I questioned why my parents insisted on teaching me a life skill I had no interest in. But life has a way of making us revisit the lessons we once dismissed.

When I moved out on my own, I realized that cooking wasn't just about making meals—it was about self-sufficiency, about taking care of myself in the most fundamental way even when I had the luxury of just hiring a cook. And yet, perfection was never guaranteed. The burnt rotis, the over-salted curries, the dishes that didn't turn out quite right—they were lessons in patience, in embracing imperfection, in finding joy even in failure.

———

"The first time I made rotis on my own, they were anything but perfect. Some were too thick, some too thin, and most had burnt edges. I stood there, staring at them with disappointment, feeling like I had failed at something so basic.

But as I sat down to eat, I realized something: the meal was still nourishing. The effort, however imperfect, still mattered.

Over time, I got better, but even now, some days, I still burn a roti or two. And I've learned to laugh about it instead of sulking. Because life, much like cooking, isn't about getting everything right—it's about trying, learning, and not being too hard on yourself when things don't turn out as expected."

—

Step by Step, Rep by Rep

For the longest time, movement was just an obligation—something I should do rather than something I wanted to do. Exercise felt like a chore, and I never truly saw it as a part of me.

But somewhere along the way, that changed. Lifting weights made me feel powerful. Yoga made me feel centered. Dancing made me feel alive. Movement stopped being about just burning calories or looking a certain way—it became my way of healing, of feeling at home in my body. In every stretch, every step, every drop of sweat, I found strength I never knew I had.

—

"There's something magical about movement—the way it shifts not just your body but also your mind. The days I feel the heaviest inside are the days I push myself to move, and somehow, with every step, every lift, every stretch, the weight in my heart feels lighter.

Fitness isn't just about aesthetics. It's about feeling strong when life makes you feel weak.

It's about proving to yourself that you can keep going, even when you want to stop. It's about realizing that movement—whether it's lifting, running, dancing, or simply stretching—isn't just about physical strength. It's about resilience. It's about healing. It's about reminding yourself that you are capable of carrying yourself forward, no matter what."

———

Part 5

Home Is Where I Am

Home isn't always a place; sometimes, it's a feeling, a person, a fleeting moment of peace within yourself. This section is about the beauty of unplanned experiences, the quiet joy of discovering comfort in unexpected places, and the journey of becoming your own safe space.

It's about finding warmth in solo adventures, in strangers who become stories, in music that makes you dance alone, and in the realization that you carry home within you—wherever you go.

Sometimes, the most profound moments of belonging come not from what we planned but from what we allowed ourselves to embrace. This is about letting go, leaning in, and trusting that life will surprise you in the best ways.

A Tattoo, an Accident & a Mother's Love

Love often reveals itself in the smallest gestures—in moments that may seem ordinary but carry extraordinary meaning. After an accident left you shaken, your mother, in an unexpected act of love, took you to get your first tattoo that you have been thinking about since days. It wasn't just ink on skin; it was her way of reminding you that pain can be transformed into something beautiful.

This is a story of maternal love, quiet understanding, and the unspoken ways in which our parents hold us when we need them the most.

—

"Some gestures are loud, wrapped in words of reassurance and grand practices. But some—perhaps the deepest—are quiet. They show up not in elaborate speeches but in the simple act of taking your hand and leading you toward healing, even when they don't have the words for it.

The day I got my first tattoo wasn't just about body art;

it was about reclaiming something after a moment of pain. It was my mother's way of saying, 'If life leaves a scar, you get to decide what it turns into'.

She never told me she understood how I felt. She didn't try to reason with me or tell me to move on. Instead, she took me to a tattoo studio, sat beside me as the ink settled into my skin, and let the moment be what it was —a quiet transformation.

That day, I learned that healing isn't always about fixing something. Sometimes, it's about turning something painful into something you can carry with pride."

—

Magic of One-on-One Conversations

There's something sacred about one-on-one conversations—the kind where time slows down, where words feel weightier, and where walls quietly fall away.

These conversations have led me to some of the most meaningful connections in my life, including my partner. This is a reflection on the depth, beauty, and life-changing magic of truly being seen and heard.

———

"I have never been one for crowded rooms or surface-level exchanges. My favourite moments in life have always been shaped by deep, unfiltered conversations—the ones where two people lean in, unafraid to be vulnerable, unafraid to truly listen.

It's in these moments that friendships are built, love stories begin, and souls recognize each other.

I met some of the most beautiful people in my life

through conversations like these. My partner was once just a stranger, someone I might have passed by if not for a shared moment that unfolded like a quiet revelation. One question led to another, one shared experience became a bridge, and before I knew it, a connection had taken root.

We often think of love in grand, cinematic ways. But sometimes, love begins with a conversation—a simple, heartfelt exchange that lingers long after it ends."

———

Balcony Performance

Loneliness and solitude are not the same. One aches; the other soothes. One evening, standing on your balcony, you heard music drifting in from another home.

You let the melody guide you, dancing alone yet feeling anything but lonely. This is a story about learning to enjoy your own company and discovering the quiet joy of being with yourself.

———

"There was a time when being alone felt heavy—like an emptiness I couldn't quite fill. But that evening on my balcony, something shifted.

A song floated through the air, coming from a home I didn't know, from people I would never meet. And instead of feeling distant from them, I felt connected. I let the music wrap around me, let my feet move, let my body sway, and suddenly, I wasn't just standing there—I was dancing.

No audience. No partner. Just me.

In that moment, I realized solitude isn't about being without people. It's about being with yourself in a way that feels whole. That night, I didn't need company. I had the music, the wind, and a heart that was learning to be at peace in its own rhythm."

———

A Hike in Chappals

Some things are best unplanned. What started as a random decision to walk toward a small hill turned into an adventure that left a lasting mark.

Along the way, you met strangers—a mother and her son —who invited you to watch the sunset with them. This is a story about spontaneity, human connection, and the beauty of unexpected friendships.

—

"I hadn't planned it. I was sitting in my apartment, staring at the hill in the distance, and before I knew it, I was walking toward it in my chappals.

I wasn't dressed for a hike. I didn't have a plan. But life doesn't always need one.

Somewhere along the way, I met a hiker mother and son duo, and they asked me if I'd like to join them to watch the sunset from the top. I could have said no, could have let hesitation win. But I said 'yes'.

And that yes led me to one of the most peaceful
moments of my life.

67

We sat there together—strangers, yet not quite. The sky
changed colors, the air grew cooler, and in that stillness,
I realized that some connections, no matter how brief,
stay with you forever."

——

One Ticket, Countless Realizations

Traveling alone is a lesson in courage. Your first backpacking trip on New Year's wasn't just about exploring a new place; it was about facing your own fears, stepping into the unknown, and learning to love your own company.

This is a reflection on the freedom, fear, and unexpected joy of solo travel.

—

"There's a unique kind of freedom in being in a city where no one knows your name.

I spent that New Year's wandering through a hill station, walking through markets, eating alone at cafés, and letting the silence between moments speak for itself.

At first, it felt strange—almost like I had forgotten how to exist without someone to talk to, without a schedule to follow. But then, something shifted. The unfamiliar streets became familiar. The solitude became comforting. And I realized that, for the first time in a long time, I was completely present.

People talk about solo travel as an act of bravery, but I think it's an act of self-discovery. Because when you're alone, there's no one else to define the experience for you. It's just you, the road, and the quiet realization that you are enough."

———

Beats Over Blues

Music has a way of freeing us, of making us feel weightless, of reminding us that sometimes, we don't need words to express joy. My discovery of EDM (Electronic Dance Music), wasn't just about a new genre —it was about movement, about losing myself in the music, about finding my happiness in the most unexpected things.

———

'I was never someone who truly *listened* to music. I picked songs with upbeat rhythms, ones that matched the steps I had learned as a child. Music was just background noise to movement, never something I paused to feel.

But then, I found EDM. Or maybe, EDM found me.

It wasn't just about discovering a new genre—it was about surrender. About letting the music take over, about feeling the bass in my bones, about losing myself in something bigger than words. It was the kind of freedom I didn't know I needed—the kind that made me feel weightless, alive, unburdened.

Music has a way of unshackling us, of filling spaces we didn't realize were empty. And in its beat, I found something unexpected—happiness, in its purest, most unfiltered form."

—

An Unscripted Ending

If there's one thing life has taught me, it's that no matter how much you plan, life has its own plot twists. Some are beautiful, some are chaotic, and some make you wonder if the universe is running low on original ideas. But through it all, I've learned that the best moments are often the ones I never saw coming.

For the longest time, I tried to follow the script—the one written by expectations, traditions, and the occasional unsolicited advice from relatives I barely know. But somewhere along the way, I realized that the most fulfilling stories aren't the ones that go exactly as planned. They're the ones that surprise you, challenge you, and make you laugh at how absurdly unpredictable life can be.

So, as I close this book, I know one thing for sure—I'm not closing the story. I'm still looking forward to writing more unscripted chapters, still waiting for the next unexpected adventure, and still excited for all the things I haven't planned yet. Because if life has taught me anything, it's that sometimes, the best plan... is having none at all.

—

9 789369 536146